WITHDRAWN

The Invented Child

The Gerald Cable Book Award Series

The Invented Child

Margaret Mackinnon

Silverfish Review Press
Eugene, Oregon

Published by

Silverfish Review Press
PO Box 3541
Eugene, OR 97403
www.silverfishreviewpress.com

Distributed by

Small Press Distribution
800-869-7553
spd@spdbooks.org
www.spdbooks.org

Library of Congress Cataloging-in-Publication Data

Mackinnon, Margaret.
  [Poems. Selections]
  The invented child / Margaret Mackinnon. -- First edition.
    pages cm
  ISBN 978-1-878851-62-8
  I. Title.
  PS3613.A27348I58 2013
  811'.6--dc23

                    2012046747

9 8 7 6 5 4 3 2 First Printing
Printed in the United States of America

Contents

for Hannah and for Bob

and in memory of my mother,
always first reader

It could not be dangerous to be living
        in a town like this, of simple people,
who have a steeple-jack placing danger signs by the church
while he is gilding the solid-
        pointed star, which on a steeple
stands for hope.

                    −Marianne Moore, "The Steeple-Jack"

I. Gauguin in Kansas

Folk Tale

after a traditional Japanese story

He knows she must have been a bird,
the same white crane he saved,
returned to flight. And now she has returned to him.
As wife. At night, he brings his face
near hers to watch the unexpected sheen,
white on white, her skin against the pillow.
And when she slowly combs her tangled morning hair,
her lifted arms seem to him like wings.
Once he found a feather on the stair.

Her husband is to her the sea.
He tastes of salt, his unwashed hair
a net that holds an ancient, briny catch.
In sleep, she breathes him deep.
And flies. She sees the coast,
sees the way the sun breaks waves
to shards of purple, gold, and rose.
She sees the squares of planted rice
serene beneath a muted glaze.
She finds a perch within the darkness of the trees.

They love their simple life, their house.
A flowering branch. A lacquered box.
Life comes to life when juxtaposed.
Each meal they share seems an emblem of the past.
A bit of rosy fish curls shyly on a tray.
A boiled custard in a plain white cup
nearly overflows like the moon's white light
inside a narrow room. They drink their tea
in somber bowls, neither green nor gray.
Like two old friends, they tell each other tales,
but never once their own—
the startled hunter, wedded to his prey,
the wounded bird, would-be wife...

But should a traveler someday pass
beyond their gate, the scene he'd see
could bring to mind a half-remembered song,
could bring to mind a Master's inky wash
wherein a single tree, a stone, a stream
find a home within an emptiness.
The painting's untold story feels like home.

Sleeping Innocence

after a photograph by Manuel Alvarez Bravo

From the dust of these mango-littered streets,
the vision of the sleeping girl rises.
Her body is a cool white scar.
Cactus quills prick the air around her.

The vision of the sleeping girl rises,
and the land's green edges draw back.
Cactus quills prick the air around her.
Each stone casts its own clear shadow.

The land's green edges draw back
as light falls on the girl, evenly as rain.
Each stone casts its own clear shadow.
A white sun shines like a spun-sugar skull.

Light falls on the girl, evenly as rain,
and we, the spectators, must hurry past.
The white sun shines like a spun-sugar skull.
The naked girl wears her good name like a garland.

We, her spectators, must hurry past,
wondering, How long has the girl been sleeping?
She wears her good name like a garland,
though all who see her take something of her beauty.

How long will the girl go on sleeping
in the dust of these mango-littered streets?
All who see her take something of her beauty,
her body, that cool white scar.

Gauguin in Kansas

The local objects of a world without a foyer

The painting draws
these farmers' wives,
thick as butterflies,
their summer cottons

bright as summer air.
Curious how the painted girl
returns the local
in her placid face,

the brown foot
of any landlocked child,
the scrap of white she clasps
in ringed fingers

rendered stiff as wood.
Not an artist's last letter,
nor crumpled love,
but something more

must hold her
to this middle ground,
reticent as a shell.
Her South Seas gleam,

exotic as the run
of other women's lives.
Above her fields,
their azure and alfalfa,

her dress is the red smear
of a rose Kansas moon,
all the fruits of night
gathered in its folds.

An Afternoon During a Time of War

at the Freer Gallery, Washington, DC

In Hokusai's *Amida Waterfall*,
a last afternoon goes on forever.
The curious blue eye of the water's source
invites inspection. The leaves are tiny tints,
unfurled. The picnickers on the ledge
do not heed any other sky.
They want for nothing.
One imagines delicate blue branches
etching the rim of one man's cup.
Their rough bronze teapot will endure.
Outside, helicopters ply the springtime streets
with news of war. Images of a burned boy.
And those who have twice
lost paradise rest awhile, here,
on the light-struck grass,
their small prayer rising in cloudless air.

Gingko Leaves

Kanazawa, Japan

Once, unexpectedly, you came at night,
pressed into my hand a yellow gingko leaf,

its parallel venation a primitive form.
Your finger traced the lines of leaf and palm

and I took pleasure in the unevolved.
I loved this leaf-map, this serious design.

We walked where yellow-layered gingko leaves
filled the sidewalk's curve. They rested

in a splatter of autumn rains,
like an overlay of outstretched hands,

fingers scarcely touching, not yet intertwined.
Once, we moved in tandem, the same

branched coursings, a parallel of line.
Now, near the rust-colored tea shop,

gingko leaves glitter on a cold morning,
gold traces of a distant time.

Incidents of Travel

*I am now an old man, over eighty-four years of age, and I have
lost my sight and hearing, and, as luck would have it, I have
gained nothing of value to leave my children and descendants but
this true story, and they will presently find out what a wonderful
story it is.*

—Bernal Díaz del Castillo

They had never seen men such as we are,
nor had they ever seen horses.
The people believed we had come from far
beyond where the sun rose to rule, and more,
that we were those of whom their gods had spoken.
The Great Montezuma himself came to welcome us,
beneath a canopy of green feathers, offering a token
for Cortés, a necklace made of golden crabs—marvelous!
—and Montezuma placed it round the Captain's throat.
Mexico was enchanted, as in the legends of Amadis,
and our soldiers wondered if the white city, the floating
beds of roses, the canals and palaces were a dream. But it was
not a dream, though you may wonder at what I say.
Of the splendor I beheld, all is overthrown today.

Montezuma had many mistresses, two great
Cacicas as wives. He was slender, neat, and clean,
fond of bathing in the afternoon. I have heard it said he ate
the flesh of young boys, but only the lean
meat of arm or thigh. At mealtimes, humpbacks and buffoons
charmed the grave ruler, and Montezuma smoked
tobacco from a tube. The witty jesters left the room
while Montezuma slept. Once, Cortés asked to look
at the highest temple and the gods: Huichilobos, god of war,
and his brother, Tezcat, god of hell. Precious stones,
gold and pearls adorned the monstrous gods, and more
gold gilded snakes they held. In the oratory, we were shown
an idol, where hearts were sacrificed to bring the people good.
But I do not remember its name, only the altar crusted with blood.

Child Dressed as an Angel

after a photograph by Graciela Iturbide

Not an Angel of the Lord, surely,
though it is her wings you notice first:
their clean, spiraling lines
like a shell left behind in a landscape
once under water.
The glittered cardboard star on her forehead
shines. All other light
seems condensed in her innocent shadow.
Hers is an imagined world,
though the desert air around her could be
sweetened with the real scent
of sage and creosote
after heavy summer rain.
If the trail she is climbing were a metaphor,
it would be unmarked.
This black-and-white is too steady,
too even for her insistent gaze
as if she might confess to some vision
of another world, one suffused with green,
as if she might see
bits of green light falling at her feet—
and you think of a tree
in a Gulfport park, once, that seemed
brilliant green under a new May sky
until what looked like leaves were birds,
small, wild parrots clustering the branches.
And in an instant,
they ascended in a massed green flight,
a sweet, surrendered whirl
of pure color,
as if the leaves themselves were rising.

Grandmother's Story

Rings of azaleas crowd the house,
magenta rising to clapboard white.
The porch winds its way like a river.
A woman is framed in the upper-story glass.
Now if the dog next door doesn't bite the girl,
I'll tell you how her hair turned pink.

The girl is dark, but favors the pink
of camellias spotting the grass. Inside the house,
the woman concocts new stories for the girl,
resting in her wrapper, snowy white.
Now if the birthday diamond doesn't turn to glass,
I'll tell you where the mermaid hides in the river.

The dark girl wades along the river,
imagining mermaids, following a pink
and silver fish, rainbowed like the glass
prisms dangling in the musty woman's house.
Now if the grandmother's sheets stay white,
I'll tell you how the gardener met the girl.

Summer mornings, the woman lets the girl
brush her hair, flowing like the river,
strands of gray and silvered white,
streaming down bare skin, mottled pink.
Now if the fire doesn't burn the crimson house,
I'll tell you why the princess broke the glass.

The woman lifts the magnifying glass,
bends close to the dark face of the girl
sleeping in the parlor of the house.
The woman's eyes well up like the river.
Now if the sky tonight isn't watermelon pink,
I'll tell you about the angel in white.

The dining table is draped in white.
Magnolias float in a cut-glass
bowl, their fragrance filtering into the pink
of evening light. The woman awaits the girl.
Now if the ugly boy doesn't dive in the river,
I'll tell you about the queen's new house.

The woman takes long white naps inside the house.
Now if the murky water turns clear as glass,
she will dream under water she is the girl.

Driving Past the House of Snowflake Bentley

*W. A. Bentley, 1865-1931, was a Vermont farmer who perfected
the art of photographing snow crystals.*

He could have had the manners
of a man who married late,
or not at all. A small man,
childless, a favorite uncle.
He played clarinet in the village band.
A little queer, a little cracked,
the neighbors said. And everything
in that life seemed touched
by light: the vague half-light
of a January afternoon,
the fields made smaller by the cold
when his world must have seemed
cornerless, cleansed,
and a pale sun shone on the black sleeve
of his one black suit, the buttonless coat,
on the black board he'd hold to wait
for the one exquisite flake
to photograph
the unfolding, six-armed architecture
of snow. When it was gone,
just that much beauty gone, he wrote.
His one ambition to preserve; his tools,
the turkey feather, broom straw.
The camera his mother bought.
The patient hand and eye.
For 47 winters, to record the snow,
each time
a wonder in what seemed
white and nearly weightless and always
new—
the way new words undo those words
we think we know.

He had that faithfulness that love demands
though he lived alone, of course,
in the house partitioned oddly
for the families on the other side.
I imagine his rooms as always cold,
low and a little sooty
on the long, slow nights;
the chemical air of developer.
I imagine the sheet music,
the scattered books, the clothes.
Once, a little sleet scraped against his window,
washed the pane with ice.
He etched a woman's name there,
Mina—
and sat where he looked out on dark trees,
the dark moon, the darker night.

Though perhaps I haven't seen it right.
Perhaps there was no sadness in the bed
untouched by love, the photographs he'd take
of young girls' smiles.
Forgive me my assumptions.
I only know his hills in summer,
washed in a thousand shades of green,
not white—
the August nights we'd wait and watch
Jupiter rise in a straight line with the moon,
another pattern that redeemed our world
from randomness.
Devotion, you said, when I asked
what love meant. Then Psyche
spent her long hours sorting the seeds,
and Bentley noted the weather on his last afternoon,
Snow flying—
Then the high, dark hills rise above us
with their paired, brave lights.
Then the heart—
its infinite and intricate discernments.

On Reading Rilke's "Blue Hydrangea"

For him, the blooms were the color
of old notepaper, or a child's faded
summer dress. I think of them
at a temple in Kamakura:
those blue ocean divers, sea dwellers,
twilight movers. Kimura-san
told stories of the women
who would come there, seeking shelter,
and the garden filled itself that day
with such clear arrangements of color:
those beautiful, showy flowers,
showering lavenders into grays,
mutable shades—
But I had misremembered.
Weren't there two temples,
Meigetsu-in, Tokei-ji?
Perhaps it was because I loved
those two ideas:
hydrangeas, *ajisai*, and that place of safety
where nothing else needed to happen—
as if love itself were a kind of idea,
green and growing,
violet, half-toned, blue.

Today, in the side yard,
our own extravagant blossoms
are cast in the clean, clear light
of early morning,
and I turn to them, the way
I first turned to you—
opening that afternoon by the North River
the way an intricate gate could have opened,
once, to a woman seeking sanctuary
in a garden of cool hydrangeas.

Little Thumbkin

Over the rim of the teacup, a tiny finger curls.
A girl emerges, her birth dress blue,
blue as the teacup's crazed blue glaze.
The mother, startled, lifts her daughter in her hand.
No other mother feels more joy!
Who could imagine such an answer to her prayers?
The air shimmers as this miracle unfurls.
Already she can see all their great, good times:
the rhymes she'll sing as her baby daughter sleeps,
the cradle she'll carve from a walnut shell,
the purple pansy fashioned into coat and hat.

Come, my baby, come and see this world.
She carries her daughter to the window sill.
The morning garden now stretches even to the sea.
The tree, no longer gnarled, seems to shelter with its shade
the blazing banks of roses. The lilies gleam like pearls.

This story has not been told before.
The window's glass gives back the mother's careworn face;
the daughter, fresh, clean, every hair in place—
and yet no larger than her mother's nose.
Will she grow? Who could say?
The mother knows the neighbors' whispers may be cruel.
She knows that in this story hope must rule.

This story, it is true, has not been told before.
And so, Mother, use now all your mother art:
Serve your girl a hummingbird egg for breakfast.
Follow the unexpected course of love.
Bless your daughter. Bless her tiny, uncorrupted heart.

Lament for the Room Upstairs

White curtains bloom in the afternoon quiet.
Flecks of sun light the floor.

A green spread covers the cast iron bed
like a moth-eaten apron of grass.

How many years have passed since you dreamed
of the window's stained-glass boy,

the way his beautiful hair falls forward
like a broad sable brush?

Dust lies equally on the photographs,
on the scrapbooks of yellowed clippings

pasted neatly as if the scissored past
could be made whole cloth.

The summer hours slip away.
This absence is what lasts.

One mute breeze drifts into another
as rain spots the room's high panes.

You watch the world turn wavy,
too slippery to hold.

Border Storm

Most went north to escape the storm,
though we drove into harm

by heading west
to visit your friend, a sad, fat priest

in exile by the river. His lofty gate
defended bad paintings, silver plate.

Amid the over-stuffed brocade
and bric-a-brac, he'd made

a crumbling haven, protection
from the dangers of affection.

He'd lift a piece of once-fine
china, eye its cracks as if a sign

of what could not be broken.
Each fragile, filigreed token,

gift from a former congregant,
he hoarded, chipped remnant

of what was once success.
I'd bought a scarlet dress

in the market square
of a border town nearly bare

of tourists. I pulled the red folds over my head.
You liked the way I looked, or so you said.

The *señora* said she could not be sure
the dyes would never bleed, or would endure.

The priest's new garden was flattened by the rains.
The tiled roof leaked, the wet stained

the faded mansion's rugs, warped floor,
our bolted bedroom door.

Why was it no surprise
to find on the door a rite to exorcise

desire? Surrounded by the deluge,
I'd imagined love a refuge.

Now, if I had those words, forgotten, pure,
could I effect a lasting cure?

The Juniper Tree

after a story by the Brothers Grimm

A man who had lost something
and a woman who had lost something
married, and lived in a house with their child.
And after all that had happened,
after the branches outside had grown tangled
with each other, and the little birds sang
so that the air around them
echoed with their sad songs, after all
the blossoms fell, it was as if
a thousand years had passed.
And the woman took their boy, broken now,
and propped him up outside the door,
placed him in a lovely yellow chair
under the juniper tree. She tied around his neck
a carefully measured strip of cloth.
Think of it now: that ribbon,
that yoke around his throat.
Imagine her misplaced tenderness, her folly.

And this unfortunate story, this tale
of brutal love is not about you—
though there may be nights when you see the mother,
as if you've glimpsed her face from a passing car.
She stands outside, one hand lifted like a dark bird
thrown against the sky. And even as the evening air
rushes past your open window,
you know that she is frightened, now,
by all she has forgotten, or mislaid,
by the juniper tree, its wintered branches,
by the body of the boy buried there,
by the hard, bare-swept yard
as empty as a field where all the carnival rides
are packed and gone by dawn.

Mary Shelley's Dream

thou aspiring Child

When I think of Mary Shelley,
she is in a room full of windows.
It is Italy. Late afternoon.
The skirt of her white dress
dazzles with the late sun on it,
the bodice dark as a bruise in shadow.
Outside, the broad turquoise sea,
the boats lined up in neat rows
like children's toys, their dark masts
pitched above the pure frivolity
of the white-capped waves.
She will have remembered this view:
a single gull looks cool and aloof,
the sand as white as fine Italian bread.
And if it is true that we are saved
by what we can't forget,
she will have remembered
this vision of archways, corridors,
and the daughter she holds, now grown cold.
She bends over her lost child, now,
as if she could complete herself
with this sudden emptiness.
And she will hold onto this afternoon
for a long time, as if by remembering
this and *this* and *this*—
for we do not forget these dreams,
nor easily release our dead,
least of all this young woman
alone in the late Italian afternoon,
this mother to a last ship, this lost harbor.

Late December in the Forgotten Florida

They had been told of something called the world.

Far from our old snow,
where the gray waste of winter
lay at another latitude,
there was a town, so small and close
you could see no other weather coming.
What we saw was a street
sloping down to the still, unmarred
face of a lake. A few pastel houses,
their broad porches. An old hotel,
now listing recklessly,
its façade a peeling, lovesick pink—
and everywhere, everywhere
poinsettias, impatiens, camellias,
even pale roses,
masses of blossoms, masses of green
joined in the same improbable landscape.
And Bartram, the Quaker naturalist,
that flower-catcher,
knew all their intricacies:
the loblolly bay with its *thick foliage,*
its milk-white fragrant blossoms
so dense the ground around the Tree
shone silver in the light. And he wrote,
Though it was now late December,
the aromatic grove appeared in full bloom—
For him, too, the rhododendron,
flame azaleas, magnolias made
a tapestry: an infinite, endless green
as if they were elements in some story
you might choose to call a dream.
But there was another side, another story.
Somehow I remembered Italy,

the Brancacci Chapel,
the afternoon we saw the way
Masaccio had painted Eve,
the woman naked and expelled
from her own particular paradise.
The way he had painted her surprise,
her shoulders bent in grief,
her mortal body, fragile, fresh,
the aging human flesh that cannot last.
The great round O of her mouth.
The way he'd shown her mouth's dark interior,
that same black—
or so it seemed to me that day—
as the vacant shadows
drifting in between the dense screens of trees
in this other garden where we walked.

Then what are the heavenly bodies?
my sleep-washed child once asked.
It was late when we drove away from that little town,
back toward winter's emptiness,
the great affection we feel for our own lost hours.
From the car, we could see how
even in that garden,
December's long-angled light colored the long grass.

Insect Singers

In the season of cicadas and hot wind,
even by the bay the air thickened.
After last year's storm, stumps of palm
spotted the gray boulevard. And here,

away from water, thorny huisache and mesquite
were shrouded in the vague, insistent drone
the insects made. Mornings, we'd discover
a layer of cicadas littering the drive,

a Pharaoh's plague crusting the cement.
But those still alive continued to emerge
from holes that pocked the earth behind the house.
They'd been underground for years—

and like old antagonisms, will come to light.
The brittle exoskeletons crunched beneath our feet
as we spread the molt on the compost heap,
trusting what was lost to revive as green.

When Her Father Wrestled with the Angel

*In the summer of 1859, preparing for his raid on Harper's Ferry,
the abolitionist John Brown lived with his followers on a farm
in Maryland.*

Years after her father was gone,
John Brown's daughter could remember
the way his sermons filled
the small, hot rooms,
the fire of his unfiltered light.
This man who'd memorized the Bible's
every verse, who'd failed
in every enterprise
had seen the Lord speak to him
in dreams—
A king against whom there is no rising up,
he'd rise early
and wait each day for more recruits
who did not come—
And Annie would recall that summer's
heavy air. She read the sky
as if it held a sign as fragile and as frail
as her footprint in the ash.
Those parts of her life would surely
reappear—
The shed filled with a thousand sword-tipped pikes.
The men, set free to exercise at night,
who filled the farm's far yard,
shadowed, slant,
their figures doubled in the dark.
And beyond, the thick trees
where the brown leaves of another year
still lay upon the ground. And beyond these,
the fields where other men would one day
perish in the flames. She'd write,

I was always on the lookout while carrying
the victuals across the porch,
always at my post. And that summer,
she feared a strange face at the window.
She asked to move the heavy stove upstairs.

But who could doubt her father's faithfulness?
And yet, when all the men were gone,
didn't she wander through those empty rooms,
enter her own reverie,
the house now spinning with her?
She'd look out at the breathing night,
spy a moon as bright
as her father's rigid heart.
She'd sometimes close her eyes,
the way a child whose father
dreams too many dreams
will close her eyes to his wild schemes.
She'd see another house, then,
one grown wide and safe around her,
imagine a different morning
coming with its half-gray light,
a morning not yet cool and blue
around its edges—
and see another sun just rising,
illuminating an entirely different room.

II. Near the Water's Edge

For My Father, Buried Under Other Trees

Maxton, North Carolina

Here, where the light slides down the knobby pines,
the bare sandy soil nearly shines in this hot

midsummer glare. The air is quiet above the graves.
They are all buried here, my high-minded

ancestors, all except my father—
apart from his young mother, who died

two weeks after he was born.
My father believed she held him close,

if only once before she died—
And since this is now my story, too,

I give him this: a warm dark, rich and curious,
and the way she could have opened her gown,

let the night breeze play across her breasts,
under her arms. No harm can come to them.

In other rooms, others are asleep, but in their quiet,
broad-porched house, they are alone in their sweet drowsing,

celestial and unencumbered—
I dreamed, once, of a boy who died just after

learning his first word: *song*. Not that my father's
long life would have ended, but that their separated lives

might coincide. And there could have been music,
surely, the way there is always some third thing.

The woman. Her baby. A tune she might have sung:

There's a friend who'll show you how to go—
Jesus is the way home—

And so, the mother and her beloved boy,
together in the room's high mahogany bed,

changed by what is always changing—
Soon. So very soon. But not just yet.

Florida Outdoor Museum: Last Photographs

for my mother

Before the first blue of evening,
in the last angled shadows of palmetto
and pine, I snapped the last
photograph of you.
Before, you'd posed in the garden,
where each labeled plant
gave a name to our aimless wandering.
You wore a new straw hat,
one a child might wear,
pushed back on your small head,
your faint, frail hair.
Your grayed face filled with light.
We'd kept all day a kind of sweet,
complacent peace.
We never spoke of death.
But in this second shot,
I caught you unaware:
You round the square porch
of an early settler's house,
its peeling white the shade
of this fading afternoon.
The camera caught motion's vulnerable blur.
Your features softened.
Your fingers brushed the balustrade,
the transient fretwork of these pioneers.
A green-shuttered window rose behind you
like an eye.
And though I cannot see it here,
the air around you filled
with the insects' dizzying hum.

Near the Water's Edge

Jesus said to them, "Come and have breakfast."
−John 21:12

In the original, it is a sea—
though I've imagined a lake in some sheltered Southern landscape,
where a mist lifts above the still cool surface of the water, slightly
　　furred.

For me, the trees near the water's edge must be pines, tall and black,
　　sap-filled,
rising up the early morning sky. The smells are late summer.
The lake will still be dark, tea-colored, with the strong scent of tannin,

especially in the shallows. A mourning dove surprises bits of light.
In the story, a man stands on the shore, though at first, the fishermen
　　in their boat
do not know him. They are tired. Their net lies empty until he speaks.

Then they lean into their work, slip the net's grave knots.
Then the oily fish roil the waters at their feet.
And one of the fishermen is Peter. A tall man, a line between the water
　　and the air.

His sun-strained eyes. The bristled hair.
It is Peter who finally recognizes the Lord, jumps into the lake, wades
　　to shore
where Jesus has built a small fire on the beach, on the damp, coarse-
　　grained sand.

Bring the fish. Come and eat.

This is the landscape of my father. His yellow pines. The single
　　mourning dove
I remember from every childhood visit to the little town where he
　　was born.
This is his August. His flat, sandy soil. And this is the landscape
　　where my father,

a fatherless, motherless child, brought his own children
to camp, to gather around our own small fires in early morning.
As in an old snapshot, the colors now are slightly blurred,

though all of us are there—
Our light sweaters, even in late summer. My brother and sisters.
Our damp socks. The chilly air—

And of all the apostles, my preacher father loved Peter best—
the flawed man who was forgiven—
though I never heard him tell this tale.

Still, there is something in its hopefulness that makes it his.
My father, the orphaned boy with a wide, endless, ever-pleasing grin.
A man who drank. A man restless, restless for what he always
    seemed to miss,

for what none of us could give. And surely this is his story,
with its odd clarity of early morning, the gray light across the water,
the drift and gathering of the waves around the sturdy fishing
    boat—

and Jesus offering breakfast on the shore, the way my father fed us
eggs he'd cooked on the Coleman stove only he could master.

One Thanksgiving

I have tried not to be troubled
by these inaccuracies:
the lawn may already have been
a mass of flat, straw-colored grasses,
lifeless under early frost;
and inside the house, the awkward,
embarrassed gestures
of my father's generosity,
once again gone slightly wrong.
A prisoner in our house.
But it was only a sad country man,
a county jail—
some minor crime, some Southern custom
of work release. And my father's idea
to invite this family, wife and son
to share dinner together—
And what then happened to them?
Was it only a short while before they moved away?
The sad man, his shy boy, about my brother's age.
The tired wife who would not meet my mother's eye.
We left them in our house that afternoon,
something about a little time for themselves,
my father said—
I think my father feared the ordinary life.
He looked for the extravagant act—
and yet he also hoped to give that man
some happiness,
the way a good dream can seem
you have been visited by so much joy.

Once, in a Dust Bowl story,
under a black sky, a furious wind,
another father picked up a woman
and her child and put them in the car

and drove away. Because the woman feared
the world might end that day
and did not want to face it down alone.
I think my father understood the embarrassment
of disaster, something I can know
without completely knowing him.

And all that happened long ago.
Before his failed heart,
before the long decline, the bottles
my mother said were found in the last desk drawer.
Let light perpetual shine upon them,
the prayer book says. I remember that light,
the bright high silence of a late November sky,
clear and infinite,
that Thanksgiving afternoon we drove away.

Unpacking My Mother's Things

In the small back room, another cool blue morning.
The begonias my husband planted
offer the clear pinks of childhood through every screen.
I sit in an old kitchen chair,
drawn from this labor of loss
to the light rising over the neighbor's wall.
Sparrows descend on the lawn.
Cardinals squawk from the wet bamboo,
bits of red among that dense, expressive green.
Last night, I dreamed again of you—
as you were almost before I knew you—
fresh, tanned, a long athletic beauty,
before illness turned your skin
so thin it shattered, actually, fragile as glass.
In the dream, I still needed you.

Take the map, you said. *Look for the street called Nuance.*
And I think of how even the slightest shift
can sway a flawed day, a sorry season.
How, for example, the swift lift
of the yellowed locust leaves can presage
rain, the close of the hot, pressed dream
of another summer afternoon. Or the way
the bright July light of your last mornings
could have seemed not melancholy, really,
but gold in its mild, spellbound impermanence.

Soon This Small Night

for my mother

Soon this small night
may be forgotten. The way
the moon rose, a thumbnail sliver,
pale and then paler,
notched against the sky. The way
a breeze stirred the palm fronds,
their *clack, clack, clack*
at the far edges of the yard.
And the hard afternoon
that brought you from your room,
your chemical-laced restlessness,
to join us near the blue TV
where we watched a woman sing
Love if you can—
It would rain by morning.
You would soon be leaving.
But for now, the woman sang
May it last forever—
And it seemed as if something undone
had its own undoing, as if pain
could nearly lift and drift
out on the sodden air,
out on the scents of salt and flowers,
out to where an egret stalked the perimeter
of the aqua pool, a chalk white
stark against the blurred water—
a specter, almost,
emissary sent from another world.

III. The Invented Child

My Grandmother's Chinese Bowl

for Hannah

Under the unshadowed sky,
its suspended V of geese
flies eternally east
above a small, spare island.
Perhaps it is early spring.
The one large tree blooms extravagantly,
some tree, perhaps, like the fig
that loves the tide, the salt
of these waves, gray-blue,
paired and unwavering.
The air around the house is white as bone.
No wind stirs the tree's branches.
The one boat lies unmoored,
as if a single soul
had already set sail on the cool, fishless sea.

You slept that first night I knew you,
my Chinese child,
in a hotel room lit by an unfamiliar
moon, one arm flung wide
in the expansive gesture of a dancer.
Your other fist clenched tight.
You seemed, even then,
as fierce in your will as any warrior.
All night, I leaned over your sleeping self,
watched your perfect face,
your smooth flesh the color of wheat,
beautiful, especially,
in the angled light of early morning—
that first light just the shade
of the one bright peony
I'd seen on the Summer Palace grounds,
the flower claiming its place

by a carved gate, already enthroned.
They say some Chinese porcelain
is made of water from a single source,
allowed to dry in sun and wind
for a long generation,
then buried in the earth for a hundred years.
We want for our children all
we love—
and what I wish for you
is this sweet amplitude:
some scene in full summer,
like that one hushed evening
we sat together on the grass,
watching our backyard fireflies—
the way their gleam weaves
an unnamed constellation
high among our familiar trees,
with just enough light
to guide the sailor in her little boat
across the clear, uncharted water.

Just Past Signal Knob

Late on a late October afternoon,
somewhere along the trail,
you've stopped,
waiting while I make my slow way
across the rocks.
I see you now—
your jacket pale against the poplars
and the oaks,
those sturdy, ink-stroked trunks,
your bright hat a match
for the thrust of rust-colored leaves,
the bright, rough flags
of another season—
and in these deep woods,
there is nothing for me
more beautiful
than the ease with which you bend
and break and make
a kind of crutch,
a crooked walking stick for me.
An early moon has risen
above the brown grass.
It is cold and nearly night now
underneath the trees,
though this clearing where you stand
has freed its light—
steel blue and what seems
a new, almost golden green
float the grave, unbroken scene.
The Japanese painter Buncho wrote,
The authentic view must be just like this.
We kiss We follow the easy path
back to where we've parked the car,
the two slopes behind us like bodies now,
waited and resting,
bowing low to the other in the not-yet dark.

Writing on the Window

a silver gleaming in the west called us to proceed
—Sophia Hawthorne on her wedding day, 1842

In their myth of middle-aged love,
they traveled down a long lane
lined with black ash trees, toward
something like paradise—
if only for a season. Soon,
it would be full summer.
And with all the windows open,
the rooms of their rented house
showed gold, a neighbor said.
In the high study upstairs,
these two, joined in their wariness,
looked out on a night capable,
it seemed, of such conciliatory brightness—
Sophia scratched with her diamond on the glass,
on the gold light
The smallest twig leans clear against the sky.

That July, the yard behind the house
was wide as Hawthorne's old dream of the sea.
The invalid artist. Her husband who brooded
on the world's deep strangeness,
murky and bottomless—
how the landscape had changed for them.
The shaggy larch repeated its deep greens
in the far glint of the water.
And Hawthorne kept a garden, called his plants
my vegetable progeny, loved, especially,
the yellow squash, *my round fellows.*
He found in his bride something like the moon,
that light that enters night, *his* night.
She danced for him to the tunes of their music box
until the old rooms grew too cold,

before he tried to settle all their debt
by selling apples, potatoes, even grass.

I think of all the ways we try to find
a name for love,
with our own misfit inventions:
Sophia's arm will shine in the light
when she leans on the sill downstairs
to write on the glass,
Endymion painted in this room.
Her last painting. A lost one.
Soon they'll pack for Salem.
Sophia puts away her paints.
Eden couldn't last.
But now, shaping that figure, a naked man,
won't she think, again, of her husband?
The way he lay beside her—
and will again—
the way his skin could hold the full
smell of the sun, even into evening,
the way the words on the windows are still visible.

After a Photograph by Jack Delano

Vermont State Fair, 1941

It would be too easy to say
they look like flowers—
these four girls in their nearly identical
red dresses, all shades of rose,
though, or some summer fruit
suited to a northern state,
raspberries, perhaps, or currants.
It's getting late.
They've been in the car for hours.
They've only just arrived,
their cotton skirts wrinkled with the heat
of being squeezed too tight
on a narrow seat. Behind them,
a red sign offers *Tickets*,
calling attention to itself
like another fretful child.
One of the girls has soft curls
her mother rolled last night.
Only one of them looks at us.
Her fingers worry the ties
of her new best dress.
Her face is the same faded tan,
the same farm brown
as the fairgrounds around her.
Her mouth twists, eyes
nearly shut in the hot September glare,
but even now,
her restlessness renders her
as clear to us,
and as insubstantial,
as a voice heard over summer water.
The camera's angle has cut off

the sky—
though we can still imagine
its wide, expectant arc,
all bright surface
where no clouds are visible.

For Grant Wood

The trees are mended.

A shy man seeks perfection in his art:
Across vast acres, color and shape of tidiness,
Iowa's unruly grass submits, blade by blade.
The blue of Mother's dishes tints the sky.

Across vast acres, color and shape of tidiness,
sloping rows and rectangles piece a new land.
The blue of Mother's dishes tints the sky.
Like a black quilt tied with loops of green,

sloping rows and rectangles piece the new land.
The reassuring fields of corn unfold
like black quilts tied with loops of green.
Under the artist's alchemy,

the reassuring fields of corn unfold.
Sweet clouds hover like the hands of God.
Under the artist's alchemy,
even winter's leaden skies grow bright.

Sweet clouds hover like the hands of God
as the Thirties' skylines and bread lines disappear.
Even winter's leaden skies grow bright.
A yellow hill rises, like the belly of a woman ripe with child,

as the skylines and bread lines disappear.
Iowa's unruly grass submits, blade by blade,
a yellow hill rises—
and the shy man finds perfection in his art.

A Marriage

*Henry Adams commissioned Augustus Saint-Gaudens to create a
memorial for his wife, who died by suicide in 1885. The gravesite is
located in the cemetery at Saint Paul's Church, Washington.*

Away from the glass-walled reception,
the Brazilian musicians who played *Samba Pa Ti*,
away from the caterer packing up for luck
the last frosted layer of our wedding cake,
from the friends who wish us well
in this marriage of middle age—
we wander on a late June afternoon
into the narrowing ring of a hedge,
once a shaggy yew, now newly-planted holly.
There are no living names here
nor dead inscriptions—
Here the landscape simplifies, shielded
from the other rows of marble cherubs,
the angels with triumphant wings,
the lyric headstones white as moons.
The figure here is bluer than remembered.
Its chased bronze surprises with its bright
sea-green, brighter even than our own midsummer sky—

This bronze has always seemed to me a woman
though the strong chin could be a man's.
The muscular, equivocal forearm masculine,
like its one strong hand that rests against the face.
She is seated like a sibyl who has already spoken.
The long, bare foot finds a steady place
on the rock, as if she has watched here
for a thousand years, as if we have come late
to her season
in some other world—
The other hand hides inside the folds
of her cloak, where there is the light curve

59

of a breast. Her lap is broad,
wide enough for a child
though the woman who is buried here
had no child—
One knee's been worn smooth, just the size of palm—

Henry Adams outlived his wife by years,
long enough to come here, to this same ground
where we are sitting now,
to catch some small breeze, balm
in this highest spot in the city.
In his *Education*, he never spoke her name.
No acclaim for her brilliant wit.
No mention of her muffled suicide.
Still, he wrote often of this living bronze,
how *every detail interested him*,
the closed eyes that might one day see
every change of light and shade.
Perhaps he knew that every memory
is always something we have made—
And if Clover Adams could sketch herself
on her honeymoon at sea, alone in a single bed,
wide-eyed, wrapped as in a shroud,
she could also photograph her terriers
sitting together at a table set for tea.
She could call her husband *beyond all words
and tender.* And if Henry Adams
could write of *the little crumb of love*
he had for her, he could also call her
*the one woman in the world never hollow
anywhere*—
Perhaps he understood the world's
always an unfathomable word.
And if art were a kind of resurrection,
it could redeem our loss. It would still be lost.

We sit adrift in our own joined
solitudes, and it is Saint-Gaudens,

the artist,
who draws me now—
This man of his own entanglements,
of complex infidelities, who sculpted
his wife's form, serene in profile
in his last piece, a man whose mistress
gave her face to the *Diana*, soaring
high above the world's great city.
It is his earth-bound figure that lifts
the light of this stern and beautiful afternoon,
his shifting angles that earn descending grace.
Henry Adams had insisted *This figure is sexless*—
But as Saint-Gaudens has made her here,
she is all body in this world where we live now,
this place where he wrote *Love*
and courage are the great things.
And so we'll make our way as best we can.
And so the ring of hollies casts a thin shade
on this monument he has made to what has ended
and to what it could have meant, this marriage
the artist imagined here—

And perhaps it is true
that all our marriages are imagined,
a story we tell ourselves,
the sweet opacities of all our second chances—
So I will think of these pairs
on another afternoon
that will be all our afternoons,
when the air is warmer still,
when we climb from our boat
on a river that shines like burnished bronze.
The day will turn at last to its own resources.
The cormorants will be another dark curve,
black as bees,
floating on the pollen-flecked face
of the water. And your freckled shoulders
are the speckled bark of the sycamore,

and I can love you there,
there in our marriage,
even in the valley of shadows,
under the fair, fading arch of the river birch.

Flora

Suppose a man could eat
that goat? the stranger asked.
But you would not sell.
Instead, the old nanny
followed you like a lovesick girl,
her coarse hair a white, spiky
radiance in the late June light.
And the night she disappeared—
you would have had a beer,
like the old Chinese poets
who drank their wine
and watched their woods.
Your woods were changing.
The heavy summer rain had cast its spell,
the grasses, the ginseng,
the beautiful sassafras all so green
they were almost blue. And you
followed her past any fear
of darkness, past Mamaw's Lake,
past the sober outcropping,
wearing your headlamp
like a miner following gold—
until she is suddenly there:
a miscreant creature
as real and dreamlike
as a sleepwalking child.
You brought her back as if
she were something
that could never be lost in this world,
as if this is what men do.
I had wanted to write about your goodness.
And I thought of Flora
when we woke today at the cabin
above Passage Creek,

where a morning branch
stretched out across the blue expanse
of valley, the pine's
small, dark cones like the negatives
of last night's longest stars.

My Mother's Photographs

perceiving, if only through the camera, some of their haunting charm—
                              –Clarence John Laughlin, 1948

In a city where I've never lived,
my mother lived—
and photographed the winter streets
of the French Quarter in New Orleans.
Such tender watchfulness in her young eye.
In the distance, a tree she saw
reaches upward and dissolves,
its tropical leaves pale streaks of gray.
The cars of the 40s are all round shapes and chrome.
She captioned these images she kept
in a worn envelope—
Galatoire's—we had trout marguery ici,
she writes. And *Arnaud's—*
shrimp—New Year's Night—
plus tarde avec Ray—
It is night and will always stay night
in her photographs,
though there is a still brightness
in these scenes of scrolled balconies,
narrow roads shiny and slick in the rain and dark.

Clarence Laughlin photographed New Orleans,
his images of women the age
of my young mother, I suppose.
They are always slim and lovely, these girls
placed in his dreamscapes amid the ruins
of perilous galleries and broken doors,
or among the white stone monuments
he called *the cities of the dead.*
Laughlin once said his pictures opened
the dark mystery of time, the luminous
mystery of light. In one,
the woman is an elegant profile,

posed the way my mother would have posed,
above a crumbling arch. Her hand
rests on a jut of brick.
She stands against a background of clouds
like a ship's figurehead,
her black dress a cool line on the rising, post-war sky.

When my mother died, I found more photographs:
images of a man handsome in a way
different from my father—
There are four, each one torn
with a raw, white edge, or scissored neatly
as if the story surrounding him
must be cut—
In one, he wears a brown suit and smiles.
In another—
the one I imagine my mother liked best—
he is outside in white shirtsleeves,
plaid slacks, a style of the late 60s.
His face carries the lines of someone,
like my mother, who loved the sun.

And there are letters, too,
though few of them intact—
He writes, *It is a fact that I miss you*
and miss you tremendously.
He writes, *You have a free, unfettered spirit.*
And in what I guess is the last,
he writes, *I miss the sharing we did*
the past few years. Here,
among my mother's hidden things,
whatever I have from this view of her
feels innocent and inviolate—
residing in some place older
than this daylit world. We say
we judge a photograph, in part,
by the quality of its lights and darks.
My mother's darks seem dense and infinite.
My mother grows lighter and younger every day.

Landscape after Thomas Eakins

This pear tree looks silver in the morning.
This summer hill above the river
offers all consolations.
Everything I've written seems transient
before you. I imagine you now,
wild hair awry, shaggy, wet from the shower
you love to take outdoors.
Rivulets trace the contours of your skin.
How Eakins might have painted you—
Here, descending to swim in some spot
where the water spreads out
wide and flat and green.
I can see in his men the same planes—
muscle, flesh shaped the way you are—
the same tense insistence, the same languid ease.
Eakins' great friend Whitman wrote about how
Little streams pass'd all over their bodies.
These same clean lines
of shoulder and of back, of belly, hip—
soft black inks inscribed forever on my hands.

The Sensation of Sight

I have always lived in small places.
    —Harry Callahan, photographer

He photographed Lake Michigan from a distance—
and in his landscape of small-scale economies,
a man in white trunks turns away
from the woman in a black bathing suit,
the water so calm, so shallow she can stand
next to her child, who is submerged up to her
shoulders, back toward us. The child's
bright top-knot. Her mother's attentive care.
The image is a field of air. Clouds drift
in the same bleached shades as the slight,
shadowed waves on the surface of the water.
If there were sound, the high sky above them
might be filled with the wild cries of birds,
but there is only silence here—

The photographer has taken us out to the mild
line of the horizon,
let us know the clear unfolding of the ordinary.
Oh, I want them all to stay—
the mother and her daughter, the unknown man,
safe in their necessary tenderness—
this perishable world, where my daughter once said
even the smallest miracle only comes
to the one who needs it—

So I wonder what we might have needed that night
when we sat on the deck after a long, hot day
on the water—
The moon was a white surprise, slight and slippery
as those little fish that had nibbled the freckles
on your shoulders in the river's shallows.
And then we watched in a dream-like reverie

as the branch of an old oak above us
swayed in a deep, leisurely way, borne down
by the great weight of a wide-winged owl,
gliding, landing—
a brief, black silhouette illuminating
our own small bit of that evening's domestic sky.

Saint-Gaudens at *Aspet*, Last Afternoons

After he was diagnosed with cancer, the sculptor Augustus Saint-Gaudens went to live at his summer house in New Hampshire. He died in 1907.

From the porch, a surprising swath of blue
leans against the far hills, cloudless
before the evening storms.
The poplars stand erect as sentinels,
the rows of birches white as brides.
For him, the meadow would have been
this same yellow-tipped wilderness,
his wife's garden
a summer wash of color:
lily, phlox, delphinium.
He would have had this same view
of the rose-walled studio,
the doors and shutters
the cool green of winter fir.

From the porch, I imagine
he could sometimes still direct
the work of his assistants from his chair,
on his best days, scribbling notes,
on his worst, lost in the restlessness,
entering a new settlement—
The hands of this man who caught
in clay and bronze
the beautiful energy of the gesture in its making
were nearly bone now,
fragile as the bodies of small birds.
Still, everything must have looked alive to him.
I see my place clearly now, Saint-Gaudens said.

Once, in a dream, I swam in an old pool,
alone among high, green hills.

Alone, but suddenly there were others—
and there among the other swimmers
was my mother, so recognizably herself.
My mother, whom I have missed
every day that she's been gone.
I held her face in my hands.
And the bones of her cheeks were the bones
of Saint-Gaudens, the bones
of a last bronze bust
made of his face just before he died.

Hers were the same inward-looking eyes,
hooded, their same brilliant light.
She looked at me, then, but did not speak.
And Saint-Gaudens' son
remembered a long summer afternoon
when they sat together on the high terrace,
when the sun shone on Mount Ascutney,
and his father was silent for a long time.
It is beautiful, he said.
But I want to go farther away.

Meditation on Three Landscapes

i.

In the high desert, I learn the white fir
is pollinated by the seemingly empty wind.

ii.

And I remember a long night
when I met a woman who told me
her story—
the three children she'd lost,
babies born but never fully born,
nameless though they were always
surely named—
Her face as she speaks turns wild with grief.
And the art she makes is some dream
of the world's haphazard signs:
what she finds in her dense, green landscape,
the sticks she brings back,
beaver-marked, black bark against the white
inner wood, chewed to a fine grid.
She piles small, brooding stones,
ties brown feathers that float
above these indecipherable maps
of her making, each pale shadow
its own disconsolate heart.

iii.

And on another morning,
behind our house the black trees
are lace-like and specific.
The heavy, brown Chama River offers
the sharp smells of mud.
I hold a bone you've brought
from your own arid wanderings,
as if what had once been cast aside
could stay. Crusty and shadowed,

this remnant suggests a broken wing,
even an angel, our daughter says,
an outstretched, lifted hand—
something linked to how the night has given way
to this vague light above the water.

And on the long, late summer afternoons,
the *cholla* cactus lifts its long arms,
green and familiar above the red earth.
But when the plant's green boundaries
are gone, its bones are an elegant web,
its interstices startling,
remarkable and carved
as if everything we'd learned and lost
had its own abandoned beauty—
How I am surprised when cactus sheds its skin.

September on the River in Our Middle Age

for Bob

We feel the obscurity of an order, a whole—
And so the Potomac that afternoon held a yellow haze,
its flat gray-green overlaid with the light
of late summer, the trees along the shore
still leafy and expectant.
We had stopped that day at a small
bit of land where we had stopped before.
You told me someone had once named
this little island, mapped it,
this land whose shape the river
is always changing—
You couldn't recall what it was called.

I have wanted to remember how it all seemed.
The sharp, watery smells close to the edge
of the land. The vanishings up beyond,
where the river was a dark swerve, long and familiar.
I have wanted to remember the feast
you made for us—
Food cooked on a fire. Chicken and wine.
A great blue heron flew low along the bank.
I have wanted to remember watching you
beside the shallow, still river, observing
your aging. The slope of lines
that had not sloped before, the way time
will pull your beauty toward some other time.

You showed me, once, some woodcuts
done by a German artist to illustrate his idea
of *city*. In his 15th century world,
he made identical images
of walls and narrow streets and high,
crowded towers to define a concept,

though each duplicated picture was named
a different name:
Damascus, Ferrara, Mantua, Milan.
But I want to say the river was for us
that day not an abstract transience,
but ours. And I want to remember
how the ordinary light diffused
into a too-sudden dark—
Though why should night surprise us?
That evening sky may have held its color
longer than it had to—

Still, startled by the change, we had to find
our way back home—
And I remember the way the black surface
of the water summoned us,
though the line of the shore was another
disappearance. The moon nearly useless,
now invisible. And I'd like to understand
how it was when we climbed into the boat.
My own fears. The elation of uncertainty.
The way your patient eye seemed to find
the cut in the land as if by feel.
And the way our paddles were a bright,
shimmering sound in the soundless air.
And how the light of even that lightless night
became abiding, somehow sufficient.

At the Rosenbach Library:
Afternoons in the Archives

*Moore kept house with her mother, an arrangement that lasted
until the elder Moore's death in 1947.*
                    –from an essay on the poet Marianne Moore, 1887-1972

i. portrait, 1929

It could be any evening in late autumn.
Outside, in Brooklyn, the lights of the street
have nearly erased the stars. But here,
in their living room—
haven for waifs, children, animals, prisoners—
how near and far away that world is.
These two have made a kind of bright city
all their own, no less real for its artifice.
The gilt candlesticks. Mismatched family pieces
of dark Victorian wood, the kind of furniture
never really meant to be moved—
A little framed print by Durer, *who would have seen
a reason for living in a town like this.*

In the painting, the mother is a second self, solid
against the daughter's bright red coil of hair.
The carved arms of their chairs turn and twist
in an amber parallel. The artist has brushed them both
with the same corals, the same crushed velvet green.
Years later, Marianne will write, *Mother
was even dressed part of the day*—
but says her clothes felt heavy and unnatural.
But in this image, Mother is in neat black, muted,
wearing the duller colors of a female bird
who made for her child, when she had to,
a carefully constructed nest,
away from the mad father, lost husband
who was always missing—

These two abide in their hopeful aggregate
of straw, salvaged scraps of sidewalk trash,
bits of discolored string—

And Marianne will write,
Everything to do with love is mystery—

ii. early photographs and drafts

There are so many photographs of cats!
In one, Marianne holds a black creature
up under her chin, so that she must have felt
its fur against her cheek.
The over-exposed light of a lost house behind her
leaks its white onto the skin
of her small hands, the collar of her dress.
A hat, broad-brimmed and black, shades her face.

She said she liked about cats their *marvelous faculty*
for finding their way over utterly unknown ground.
And I found something she wrote
in a little notebook: *mother cats sometimes take*
strong likings to the young of animals and birds,
especially when deprived of their own offspring.
Thus, a Tabby recently took temporary charge
of six newly-hatched chickens,
carefully protecting them from harm.

When she described the paper nautilus, she focused
on the center of the poem,
worrying in draft after draft
how to name the mother,
who sheltered her unnamed eggs,
who is *hindered to succeed.*
And since I did not come by motherhood
the easy way, I need to understand
The tense mother, as she sometimes called her.

The watchful maker of it.
The watchful mother—
she scarcely leaves, she scarcely eats—

Until, at last, she writes, love becomes the only fortress
strong enough to trust to—

I did not come by it the easy way.

iii. what was lost and what could not be lost

When her mother died, Moore's brother
advised she keep an image nearby,
some photograph to recall
what was lost and what could not be lost.
This is the one she framed for the living room
in Brooklyn: near the end, they are dressed
almost identically, just as they had been
years earlier, almost like sisters,
when they wore long white dresses in the same style,
posed against the long backdrop of other summers.

Now their full dark skirts, heavy stockings
are again the same. The same lace-up shoes.
The daughter inclines her head, bird-like,
as she has done in photographs since she was young,
as if she is still listening for some word
she needs to hear—
She looks to the camera. Her mother's gaze
is soft, vague—
Marianne's arm is against her mother's arm.
Her left hand holds her mother's hand,
strong and insistent—
a child's grasp, or a mother's hold on her child.
Her mother's scarf almost floats away.

I dreamed of them once—
outside at night, in some theatrical gathering.
They are again in these same clothes, the sensible shoes.

They are walking through the dark,
happy with each other—
Each holds the other's hand.
And I think of them in a long line,
endless, really—
mothers and daughters, daughters and mothers.
Those who have made the distant heavens a home
for us—
who, we need to believe, still lovingly
hold us—
and still remember our names.

The Invented Child

I spring from the pages into your arms.

Someone who once knew him said
Walt Whitman sang before breakfast
behind his bedroom door—
broken arias, bits of patriotic tunes,
the way my child sings this morning
in early spring, the way
the raucous mockingbirds fill the warming air
with their own borrowed songs.
The world is once again its hopeful green.
Bold forsythia bursts its spindly stalks.
The young trees again flicker on the slopes,
and when he ended his days on dusty
Mickle Street, Whitman must have remembered
mornings like this—
Nights, no longer really sleeping, confined
to the paralytic chair, say he remembered
that earlier, softer air, the light on the water
in that clearing he had called Timber Creek,
the idea of it—
Say he thought again of those days
when he was still *fat & red & tanned,*
when he'd strip off his clothes
and roll his great flesh in the pond's black marl.

In the close, bug-ridden room in Camden,
he spoke, sometimes, of a grandson,
fine boy, a Southern child who sometimes wrote,
once stopped by—
No one ever saw him.
An old poet. His invented child.
Though why shouldn't a man
who'd always lived in words create something
to endure his sore, soiled world?

There, at Timber Creek, Whitman wrote about the trees,
their rough bark, the massive limbs and trunks,
as if they were the bodies of those he'd loved.
Some people believe the souls of unborn children
rest in trees. Say he saw them, then,
caught their soft breath
sweet as the spice bush, lush as the early crocus.
In the long, hard work of his imagination,
say he watched their disembodied hearts
sway among the new leaves,
watched the eager light shine on another fine morning
until the sky lifted above him
like exultant, fresh desire—
and the children descended,
and then the crowns of the trees were all on fire.

Ocracoke

for Sara

Think of the squat yellow house,
as cheerful and incongruous
as a tropical bird,
the extravagant pink crepe myrtle
in full bloom. Think of
Springer's Point, this morning's
early trail, the twisting live oak
above Pamlico Sound.
The windy yaupon, wild olive,
the black needlegrass.
Think of Chester on the back porch
with his stories of cake and fig preserves,
the milky white fig sap,
those lemon figs,
the wasps that *loved that tree*
to death—
Think of the sugar fig,
small and sweet and round.

On the last night you lived,
you said, *I'm so lucky,*
I'm so lucky—

Think, now, of the sea,
which loves what is lost.
Think of the ocean, green
and unweary,
its undulant gray and silver-gray,
the long lift and fall
that is always around us,
the bright silver-green.

Think of all you saw:
the swift white arc
of a black-tipped gull.

Acknowledgments

Delaware Beach Life: "Ocracoke"
The Georgia Review: "Gauguin in Kansas"
Hayden's Ferry Review: "Gingko Leaves"
Image: "The Invented Child"
The MacGuffin: "My Grandmother's Chinese Bowl"
The Midwest Quarterly: "Late December in the Forgotten Florida"
New England Review: "Sleeping Innocence"
Nimrod: "September on the River in our Middle Age"
Poet Lore: "An Afternoon during a Time of War," "Just Past Signal Knob"
Poetry: "Folk Tale," "For Grant Wood"
Quarterly West: "Border Storm," "Insect Singers"
RHINO: "The Juniper Tree"
Shenandoah: "Writing on the Window"
The South Carolina Review: "Flora"
Southern Humanities Review: "Florida Outdoor Museum: Last Photographs"
Sun Dog: "Grandmother's Story"
Tar River Poetry: "Lament for the Room Upstairs"
Valparaiso Poetry Review: "Mary Shelley's Dream"

"Folk Tale" was featured on *Poetry Daily* on June 24, 1998.
"Grandmother's Story" was awarded the 1992 Richard Eberhart Prize in
   Poetry from Florida State University.
"Incidents of Travel" received a 1992 Simon Daro Dawidowicz Poetry Award
   from Florida International University.
"Lament for the Room Upstairs" was reprinted in the *1997 Anthology of
   Magazine Verse & Yearbook of American Poetry*.
"Little Thumbkin" appeared in *The 2001 Emily Dickinson Awards Anthology:
   A Commemorative Edition of the Best Poems of 2001*, edited by Glenn Reed,
   published by Universities West Press, 2001.
"Ocracoke" received a 2011 poetry prize from the Rehoboth Beach Writers'
   Guild.
"Writing on the Window" received the 2012 Graybeal-Gowen Poetry Prize
   from *Shenandoah* and Washington and Lee University.

"The Way I Iome" by Kate Campbell is quoted by permission in "For My
Father, Buried Under Other Trees."

The interior text and display type were set in Adobe Jenson, a faithful electronic version of the 1470 roman face of Nicolas Jenson. Jenson was a Frenchman employed as the mintmaster at Tours. Legend has it that he was sent to Mainz in 1458 by Charles VII to learn the new art of printing in the shop of Gutenberg, and import it to France. But he never returned, appearing in Venice in 1468; there his first roman types appeared, in his edition of Eusebius. He moved to Rome at the invitation of Pope Sixtus IV, where he died in 1480.

Type historian Daniel Berkeley Updike praises the Jenson Roman for "its readability, its mellowness of form, and the evenness of color in mass." Updike concludes, "Jenson's roman types have been the accepted models for roman letters ever since he made them, and, repeatedly copied in our own day, have never been equalled."

The typeface used for the cover titles and the back cover text is Bulmer Title. The author's name was set in Bulmer Italic on the front cover. Bulmer was designed by William Martin in 1792 for the Shakespeare Press. He worked under John Baskerville, and his types show Baskerville's influence. By condensing the letterforms, giving the strokes higher contrast, and bracketing the serifs slightly, Martin made his typefaces both beautiful and practical. The award was set in Fairplex Narrow, which was designed by Zuzana Licko in 2002.

Silverfish Review Press is committed to preserving ancient forests and natural resources. We elected to print *The Invented Child* on 30% post consumer recycled paper, processed chlorine free. As a result, for this printing, we have saved: 1 tree (40' tall and 6-8" diameter), 499 gallons of water, 293 kilowatt hours of electricity, 64 pounds of solid waste, and 120 pounds of greenhouse gases. Thomson-Shore, Inc. is a member of Green Press Initiative, a nonprofit program dedicated to supporting authors, publishers, and suppliers in their efforts to reduce their use of fiber obtained from endangered forests. For more information, visit www.greenpressinitiative.org.

Cover design by Valerie Brewster, Scribe Typography.
Text design by Rodger Moody and Connie Kudura, ProtoType.
Printed on acid-free papers and bound by Thomson-Shore, Inc.